3 4028 08493 5684
HARRIS COUNTY PUBLIC LIBRARY

J 595.733 Bod
Bodden, Valerie
Dragonflies

$27.10
ocn831150552
First edition.   06/25/2014

D1776524

WITHDRAWN

creepy creatures

CONTENTS

Introduction 4

What Is a Dragonfly? 7

A Dragonfly's Life 13

Make a Dragonfly 22

Glossary 23

Read More 24

Websites 24

Index 24

Published by Creative Education
P.O. Box 227, Mankato, Minnesota 56002
Creative Education is an imprint of
The Creative Company
www.thecreativecompany.us

Design by Ellen Huber
Production by Chelsey Luther
Art direction by Rita Marshall
Printed in the United States of America

Photographs by 123rf (Adrian Hillman), Alamy (V&A Images), Dreamstime (Charles Brutlag, Cossac, Le-thuy Do, Jaroon Ittiwannapong, Niceregionpics), Getty Images (Laara Cerman/Leigh Righton, Lasting Image by Pedro Lastra), iStockphoto (Antagain, Evgeniy Ayupov, Eric Isselée, TommyIX), Shutterstock (4736202690, alslutsky, Mircea BEZERGHEANU, Vital Che, Panachai Cherdchucheep, Foxtrot101, Adam Gryko, irin-k, Eric Isselee, kurt_G, LorraineHudgins, Evgeny Parushin, Serg64, Pan Xunbin), SuperStock (FLPA, Minden Pictures)

Copyright © 2014 Creative Education
International copyright reserved in all countries. No part of this book may be reproduced in any form without written permission from the publisher.

Library of Congress Cataloging-in-Publication Data
Bodden, Valerie.
Dragonflies / by Valerie Bodden.
p. cm. — (Creepy creatures)
Summary: A basic introduction to dragonflies, examining where they live, how they grow, what they eat, and the unique traits that help to define them, such as their ability to maneuver in flight.
Includes bibliographical references and index.
ISBN 978-1-60818-354-8
1. Dragonflies—Juvenile literature. I. Title.
QL520.B63 2013
595.7'33—dc23   2013010464

First Edition
9 8 7 6 5 4 3 2 1

dragonflies

VALERIE BODDEN

CREATIVE EDUCATION

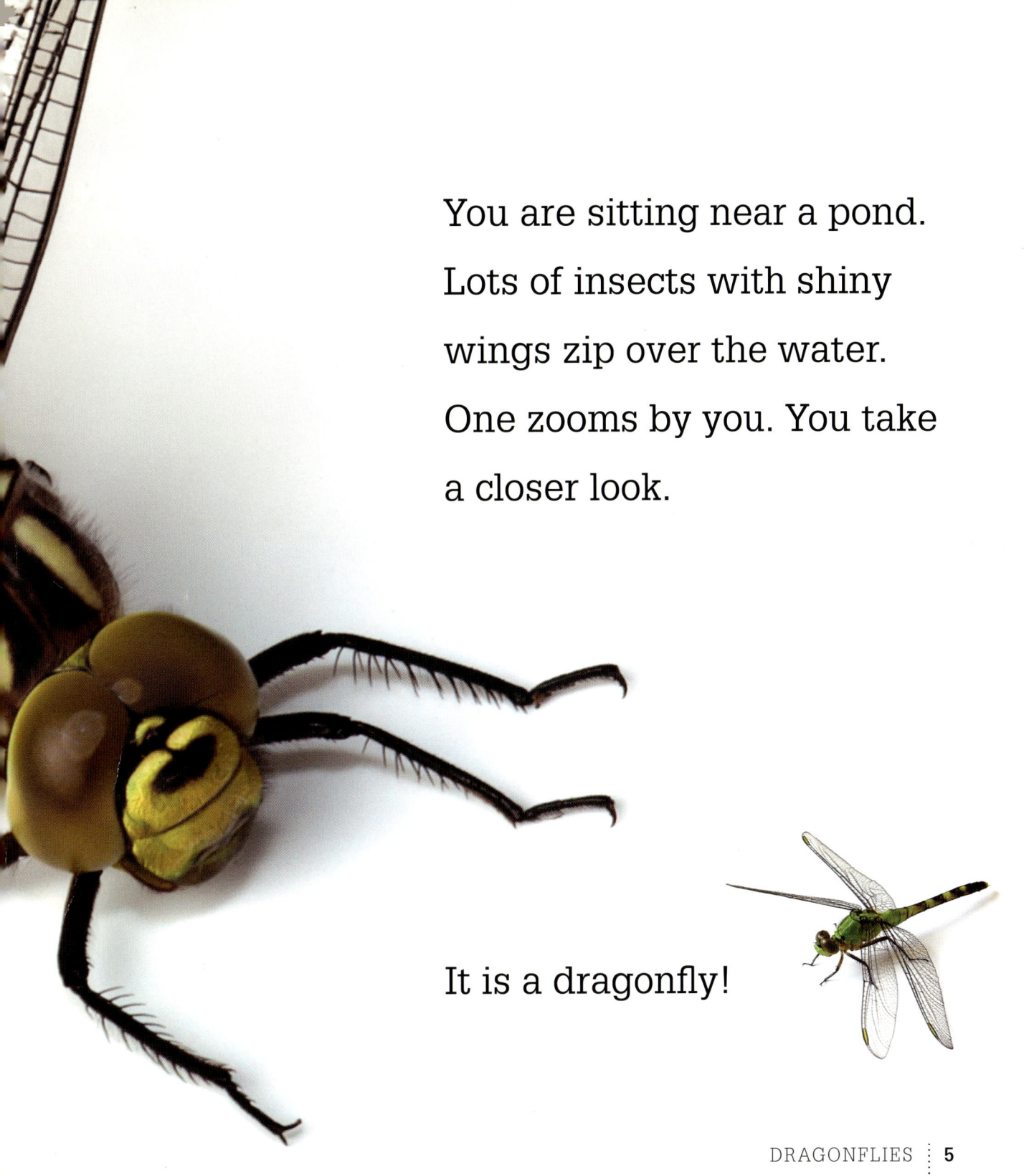

You are sitting near a pond. Lots of insects with shiny wings zip over the water. One zooms by you. You take a closer look.

It is a dragonfly!

The two large compound eyes are made up of 30,000 lenses

6 | CREEPY CREATURES

Dragonflies are insects. They have a long, thin body made of three parts. Dragonflies have six legs and two pairs of wings. They have two large eyes and three smaller eyes. Dragonflies have two small **antennae** (*an-TEH-nee*), too.

Many dragonflies have colorful bodies. They can be blue, green, yellow, or black. Some dragonflies have clear wings. Others have brightly colored wings. Some dragonflies are as small as your thumbnail. Others are as long as your hand!

Dragonflies have an average body length of 1 to 4 inches (2.5–10.2 cm)

DRAGONFLIES 9

The Halloween pennant dragonfly is active year-round in Florida.

There are about 2,700 different kinds of dragonflies. The Halloween pennant is a small, orange and brown dragonfly. The giant hawker dragonfly has the longest wings of any dragonfly. Its wings stretch six inches (15 cm) from tip to tip when they are open.

Birds and frogs have to be fast to catch a dragonfly

Dragonflies live near fresh water such as rivers, ponds, and lakes. Dragonflies have to watch out for **predators**. Birds, frogs, and fish all eat dragonflies.

A female dragonfly lays up to 100,000 eggs at a time

Dragonflies lay their eggs in or near water. A **nymph** (*NIMF*) comes out of the egg. The nymph does not have wings. It lives underwater. The nymph begins to grow. It gets too big for its shell. So it **molts**. The nymph keeps growing and molting. After about 11 months, it molts one last time. It becomes an adult with wings. Most adult dragonflies live for only one month.

Dragonflies spend their days hunting. They eat other flying insects such as flies or beetles. Sometimes they even eat other dragonflies.

Dragonflies also eat smaller relatives called damselflies (pictured)

DRAGONFLIES 17

Dragonflies are great fliers. Some dragonflies can fly 25 miles (40 km) per hour. Dragonflies can zigzag, **hover**, and even fly backward!

18 CREEPY CREATURES

The emperor dragonfly flies high in the sky to find food

DRAGONFLIES 19

People in Japan have always liked dragonflies. They think dragonflies stand for strength and happiness. In some parts of the world, people used to think dragonflies could sew a person's mouth and eyes shut. It can be fun finding and watching these fast-flying creepy creatures!

Dragonflies have been on Earth for almost 300 million years

MAKE A DRAGONFLY

Make your own dragonfly by painting a craft stick with bright colors. This is your dragonfly's body. Paint two other craft sticks a different color. When the paint dries, add some glue and glitter. Then glue the sticks together in a wide "X" shape. These are your dragonfly's wings. Glue the wings onto the other craft stick. Then add some wiggly eyes!

GLOSSARY

antennae: feelers on the heads of some insects that are used to touch, smell, and taste things

hover: to stay in one place in the air

molts: loses a shell or layer of skin and grows a new, larger one

nymph: a young dragonfly

predators: animals that kill and eat other animals

READ MORE

Helget, Nicole. *Dragonflies*. Mankato, Minn.: Creative Education, 2008.

Johnson, Jinny. *A Dragonfly*. Mankato, Minn.: Amicus, 2012.

WEBSITES

BioKIDS: Dragonflies
http://www.biokids.umich.edu/critters/Anisoptera/pictures/
Check out lots of dragonfly pictures.

Enchanted Learning: Dragonfly Printout
http://www.enchantedlearning.com/subjects/insects/dragonfly/Dragonflyprintout.shtml
Learn more about dragonflies, and print out a dragonfly picture to color.

INDEX

antennae 7

bodies 7, 8, 22

eggs 15

flying 18, 21

foods 16

homes 13

kinds 11

life span 15

molting 15

nymphs 15

predators 13

sizes 8

water 5, 13, 15

wings 5, 7, 8, 11, 22

Harris County Public Library
Houston, Texas